HALLUCINATION

THEORY

D1598501

HALLUCINATION THEORY

Published by The Reinforcement

ℝ!

www.thereinforcement.com

USA

First published in the United States of America by
The Reinforcement, 2020

The Reinforcement is a publishing company created in 2020 by
the Gold Brothers.

ISBN: 978-1-952631-00-9

Printed in the United States of America.
Set in EB Garamond
Illustrations and Cover Design by Spencer Gold

HALLUCINATION THEORY

How Hallucinations Govern Imaginations

by
Spencer Gold

R!

FIVE THINGS THIS BOOK WILL HELP YOU ACHIEVE:

1. *Develop the ability to dehypnotize yourself and others from bad hallucinations.*

2. *Nonchalantly navigate problems, create win-win solutions, and be affirmed from within.*

3. *Become conscious of unconscious processes and recognize the roles each character is playing.*

4. *Learn how to frame your experiences in the most beneficial ways imaginable.*

5. *Utilize the power of good hallucinations to improve your well-being and actualize your potential.*

Contents

Part 1:
INTRODUCTION

THE HALLUCINOGENIC REALITY

Your interpretation of hallucinations is about to change.
No drugs required.

What do the beach-goer, the thinker, the music listener, the tv watcher, and the lover all have in common? They are all under the influence of a hallucinogen.

Colors are hallucinogens. Words are hallucinogens. Stories are hallucinogens. Thoughts, feelings, sensations, the weather, environments, art, animals, even people are all hallucinogens.

Everything that you see *is a hallucinogen.*
Everything that you hear *is a hallucinogen.*
Everything that you perceive *is a hallucinogen.*

A hallucinogen is any stimuli that alters your focus of attention, thoughts, emotions, or state of consciousness.

Whenever you recall a memory from your past and are affected physiologically and emotionally, you are hallucinating. Whenever your thoughts get trapped in a negative cycle and cause you to worry about a fictitious future, you are hallucinating. Whenever *you are totally immersed in an idea — believe it, accept it as fact, make it your reality* — you are hallucinating.

You can choose to dislike the hallucinogenic effects of these stimuli, and try to resist their influence; or you can choose to enjoy and be empowered by the miracle that is the Hallucinogenic Reality.

We each co-create our experiences with the Hallucinogenic Reality. We all live in the same Hallucinogenic Reality, yet none of our experiences of it can be the same because we each perceive the Hallucinogenic Reality with our own distinct frame. Since we all have a different relationship with the Hallucinogenic Reality each character emits a one of a kind hallucinogenic stimuli.

The Hallucinogenic Reality encompasses every living entity and influences the subjective experience each entity will have.[1]

Embracing the Hallucinogenic Reality enhances your understanding of the truth because *being aware of the facade prevents you from acclimating to the facade.* With this clarifying state of mind, you will be able to see the subtle hallucinogenic effects of everyday things. You may think the mystery of the universe may diminish after discovering the Hallucinogenic Reality, but the magic is only just beginning.

Hallucination Theory provides your character with the necessary layer of abstraction to lower the stakes and improve effectiveness by turning sufferable situations into aesthetic experiences. Lowering the stakes imposed on the individual by nature and society gave birth to the achievement of civilization.

---

[1] The subjective experience that your character has determines the genre of your character's story, your inner emotional life, and your character's arc.

Refusing to accept the Hallucinogenic Reality means that you are still under the spell of the Hallucinogenic Reality.

We are not naturally built to be aware of the Hallucinogenic Reality, so we must develop an awareness of it.

Becoming a character that is aware of the Hallucinogenic Reality is a revelatory act.

WHAT IS A HALLUCINATION?

A hallucination is an idea so believable that it becomes your reality, dictating how you make sense of life and act in the world. Hallucinations control our ability to make sense of the world by framing scenarios. How we frame scenarios determines how we draw meaning from our perceptions, the meaning we draw from our perceptions determines how we respond to situations, *and how we respond to situations determines the reactions of others.* That is to say, your thoughts and feelings about others profoundly influence the thoughts and feelings others have about you.

Beliefs are ideas that your character accepts or mistakes as truth. Each belief has a stem, or core value, that it grows from.[2]

Where did those beliefs come from? Did you plant them, or were those beliefs propagated by some stranger and routinely sprayed with pesticides for years

---

[2] A belief that doesn't align with any of your core values will lack the support it needs to flourish.

without you even being aware of it? Is that very idea a weed, a bad hallucination that you keep watering and worrying about for no reason? Trying to uproot weeds that don't exist causes weeds to grow where they previously didn't.

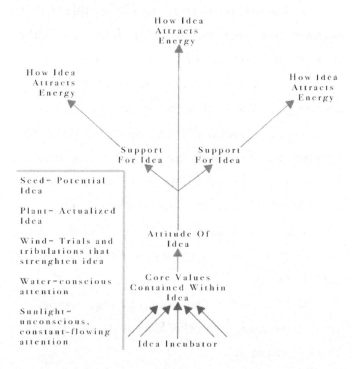

Are your beliefs serving you, or are you serving them? If your beliefs aren't serving you, you can try to uproot them and replace them with beliefs that do serve you, or you can destroy the illusion that there are weeds to uproot by identifying those weeds as bad hallucinations.

Now that you've read this, the next time you experience a bad hallucination, you will know not to react — because now you know that there's nothing to react to.

EXPERIENCING A   REACTING AS   DESTROYING THE
HALLUCINATION   PROGRAMMED   ILLUSION

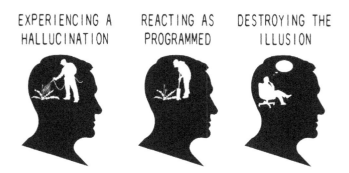

Hallucinations not only determine what we are perceptive of, they determine what we are unable to perceive. Frames[3] control what your character is selectively perceptive of and *determine what your character continually internalizes.* Your frame functions as a stimuli filter that prevents you from being overloaded with unnecessary information. Our frame determines which information is valuable,

---

[3] Frame = the hallucinogenic ideas that compose the context that your character applies to content, determining your subjective experience and mental representation of reality.

enabling us to rearrange seemingly unconnected noise into an intelligible song with a coherent story.

BAD
HALLUCINATIONS

Bad hallucinations = beliefs that you serve.

When you are convinced that something is real, when in fact it isn't, and as a result you suffer, you are experiencing a bad hallucination. Bad hallucinations cause anxiety, pain, and sabotaging self-talk. Bad hallucinations cause your imagination to work against itself.

The mere act of noticing a bad hallucination enables your character to effortlessly make a choice: cause the bad hallucination to disappear, or transform it into a good hallucination.

GOOD HALLUCINATIONS

Good hallucinations = beliefs that serve you.

When you know that something isn't real, but choose to believe that it is real anyway, when in fact it isn't, and as a result you are empowered, you are experiencing a good hallucination.

To transform a bad hallucination into a good hallucination, focus on all the instances that contradict the bad hallucination. This destabilizes the bad hallucination, taking away its power. Making a habit of focusing on these repeated contradictions makes it easier to automatically transform bad hallucinations into good hallucinations.

Good hallucinations enable you to co-create your experiences with the Hallucinogenic Reality. Just as geographical location determines a region's weather, the good hallucinations[4] within each character's frame determine how often they access beneficial psychological states.

---

[4] Bad hallucinations limit a character's access to beneficial psychological states.

THE WORLDWIDE WEB OF HALLUCINATIONS

Humanity's stability is supported by a web of hallucinations that we as a species have been weaving for thousands of years.

This web of hallucinations contains the entirety of human experience and knowledge. When we're born, each of us is randomly spit out into a different region of the web, which determines the obstacles that your character will face. These obstacles can be anything ranging from poverty, to social conditioning, to an accent.

A character can untether themselves from the web of hallucinations by rising above their frustration with how *society is built to engineer characters into certain roles*. The default role, or habitual frame, of your character will be changed just by the act of examining the region of the web that you were spat in.

Developing a sense of positional awareness automatically changes your role.

WHAT IS A MASS HALLUCINATION?

*A mass hallucination is when a swarm of characters
become possessed by one hallucination.*

When an idea becomes believable and pervasive
enough to dictate how groups of people make sense of
life and act in the world, a mass hallucination is
formed. The primary reason mass hallucinations
continue to be reinforced is because they stabilize other
hallucinations.

Rather than risk alienation, most people acclimate
and act in accordance with mass hallucinations. Most
characters remain confined inside mass hallucinations
due to the vast amount of time and effort it takes to
disprove collective falsehoods and combat shared
cognitive dissonance. It's easier to follow instructions
than it is to forge your own path.

The choice is simple: doing what's challenging is
more rewarding than doing what's easy.

HOW A HALLUCINATION BECOMES A MASS HALLUCINATION

The delivery and presentation of a hallucination decides if it gets adopted or not.

Responses to a hallucination become amplified as more people focus their attention on the same thing. As more and more characters do the same thing, it becomes more likely that others will adopt that shared behavior and acclimate to the mass hallucination. The more often characters focus their attention on the same thing, the more amplified their responses become.

Repetition amplifies selective perception.

Skeptics stop hallucinations from becoming mass hallucinations, but even skeptics often succumb to the mass hallucinations repeatedly propagated by media conglomerates. Today's schizophrenic-like media conglomerates have lost their ability to distinguish what's real and fake, and have taken away the public's ability to do so as well.

In a fury of panic to survive the rapid technological changes that revolutionized other parts of the economy, these lumbering media giants have concocted a poisonous mixture of confusion, hysteria, fear, shock, and outrage to wring out as much attention from their consumer-base as possible. This one emotional mixture gives media conglomerates the power to spawn and spread mass hallucination after mass hallucination. Media conglomerates only choose to use such toxic emotional mixtures as fuel to spread their hallucinations because that's what generates the greatest probability that their hallucinations will become mass hallucinations — all-but guaranteeing profits.

The most nefarious types of mass hallucinations condition people to desire to be conditioned; media conglomerates condition people to desire traumatic programming.[5] Out of all emotions, media

---

[5] A media conglomerate's users are like addicts that must continually consume larger doses of trauma to get their fix. Those that are traumatized often experience shame, shattering the confidence in their own perception of reality, causing them to introject and be easily misled.

conglomerates most desire their viewers to be consumed in panic — the most contagious emotion.[6]

Humans have been wired to share what they are panicking about with others, in hopes that if enough people panic about the same thing, the source of their panic will be alleviated. To stop the spread of toxic emotions, we must take action and rewire our relationship with panic. The panicking media conglomerates are incentivized to manipulate our instincts and perceptions, making it a fool's errand to try to correct them.

People consumed by mass hallucinations often experience stress, anxiety, depression, anger, and alienation. We experience stress and anxiety when we feel like we can no longer effectively cope with reality. We experience depression when we lose something of significance. We experience anger when we consciously or subconsciously observe a wrongdoing that we feel must be corrected, or if we feel that we are not being heard or understood. We experience alienation when we feel that we cannot live authentically. Those that feel that they cannot live authentically live in fear that

---

[6] Panic is a more contagious emotion than fear because panic is a mixture of fear and apprehension. If panic is not confronted, it will spawn helplessness, and helplessness will then spawn hysteria.

they will be punished for expressing thoughts that are incongruent with a mass hallucination.[7]

Feeling panicked — or paranoid — is one of the many emotions that can function as a signal informing you that you are experiencing a bad hallucination.

Be thankful that paranoia exists. Paranoia is a double-edged sword that acts as a signal to:

1. Prepare you for a looming threat, *or*

2. Awaken you to the fact that you're experiencing a bad hallucination.

---

[7] Identifying the cause of our feelings isn't always necessary. Feelings may lack a valid reason for existence, yet they may exist all the same. Even if you don't know why an emotion emerged, you can still effectively respond to it. Knowing the reason as to why an emotion emerged only serves to make it easier to effectively respond to.

STABILIZING OR DESTABILIZING

Our behaviors are reinforced because the Hallucinogenic Reality has rewarded us for those behaviors. As mass hallucinations are stabilized and destabilized over time, a behavior that was once rewarded can easily become a behavior that is punished, and a behavior that was once punished can easily become a behavior that is rewarded.

A character's self-concept does not determine their degree of success: prosperity is determined by the way that a character stabilizes their self-concept.

When a character is reinforced, validated, or rewarded for behaving in a particular way, their self-concept is being stabilized by the external world. When characters depend on the external world for stabilization, their frame becomes unstable. When the external world provides reinforcement and validation of a character's frame, they become dependent on externalities to stabilize their frame.

Characters that look to the external world to reinforce their frame are atrophying their ability to stabilize their own frame. While externalities may stabilize their pre-existing self-concept in the short term, internalizing praise from others prevents that character from independently stabilizing their self-concept in the long term.

A reinforced internal frame overcomes an external frame, even if the external frame has been reinforced more frequently than the internal frame.

A character that lacks a reinforced internal frame succumbs to the context of each situation. Gaining the ability to apply your own context to each situation makes you the author of your own subjective experience. If a character destabilizes your frame and alters your contextual understanding of your perceptions, they can influence your subjective experience. The dynamic context that your character applies in each situation is the most determinant factor of your identity.

CONTENT ×
CONTEXT =
SUBTEXT

If "content is king"[8] then context is the kingmaker.

Feelings are not what we think they are. Feelings should not be framed as primitive base instincts to be contained and controlled. Feelings are ephemeral hallucinogenic stories that are woven together whenever our character makes micro-predictions about what was and what is, and what might[9] and what will happen. *Our feelings weave the fabric of our reality.*

Whenever you make a micro-prediction, you contextualize the content of the situation, giving it a new meaning. The meaning you draw from a situation determines your response. Your response determines how others react.

---

[8] Bill Gates, 1996

[9] Before we can predict what will happen we must first predict what might happen.

Each situation supplies your character with content, and we all apply our own unique context to that content — therefore accessing a different subtext.[10]

The subtext that you access and derive meaning from determines your character's subjective experience. Knowing about the Hallucinogenic Reality is like being able to contextualize all content in a way that creates a beneficial subtext. By using color theory as a visual model, we can easily see how contents mix with contexts to create subtexts.

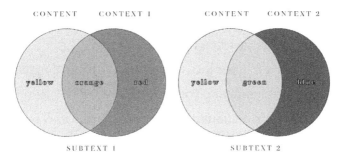

In the charts above, yellow content (perception of hallucinogenic stimuli) × red context (a negative frame of the hallucinogenic stimuli) = orange subtext (a negative response).

---

[10] To determine the truth, do your best to remove any and all contexts being applied to the content. By objectively judging the content (what happened), your subjective perception of the content (your story about what happened), is less likely to interfere with your judgement. Focusing on the objective content stops the rhetorical spinning by getting down to the facts.

Yellow content (perception of hallucinogenic stimuli) × blue context (a positive frame of the hallucinogenic stimuli) = green subtext (a positive response).

Hyper-focusing on content or subtext will cause a negative response. If you are consumed by what others are communicating beneath the surface (subtext) you will often misinterpret others as condescending, malicious, or hostile. Characters confined in the substratum of subtext see suffering everywhere, even in places where there is no suffering present. If a character gets imprisoned in the substratum of subtext they will blame others for their own self-conscious suffering, and project cruel intentions onto the innocent.

If you are hyper-focused on what is happening on the surface (content), your experience will be at the mercy of the situation that you are consumed in. Those that are confined to the surface level (content), have no desire to attempt to analyze or frame their experiences. Instead, they prefer to remain dependent on externalities to determine their experiences, causing them to be unable to see (subtext) let alone take the reins of (context) their puppet strings.[11]

By making the choice to focus on the context you apply to the content, you can transcend the assigned subtext of each situation and respond in the most beneficial way imaginable.

1. Perception of Stimuli

2. Frame of Stimuli

3. Interpretation of Stimuli

4. Meaning of Stimuli

5. Experience of Stimuli

---

[11] At times, it can be beneficial to focus on the content or subtext of a situation. Characters focus on the *content* when they desire to flow with the experience rather than analyze it or frame it. Characters focus on the *subtext* when they desire to analyze the experience rather than flow with it or frame it.

If the mind reacts to the body's cue, the body is in charge. If the mind frames the cue with a narrative that serves the character, the mind is in charge.

If the self reacts to the cues of others, then the others are in charge. If the self frames the cue in a way that serves itself and the group, the self is in charge.

Responses to a cue depend on the meaning assigned to that cue. For example, when someone else causes us to react, we can take one of two approaches:

1. Attempt to control our thoughts and emotions and be displeased with ourselves if we happen to lose control. (Unhealthy frame) *or*
2. Believe that the more we are affected by the external world, the more empowered with energy we become. The more energy we are

empowered with, the better our response will be. (Healthy frame[12])

While the event remains the same, the meaning drawn from the event changes drastically. Since *the second frame is more beneficial* than the first frame, *the second frame is stabilized, internalized, and reinforced.*

Others do not perceive what you internalize and absorb, they perceive what you reflect and refuse to absorb. The grass is green because it absorbs every other frequency of light besides green light, which it reflects. Before you can can apply beneficial frames, you must *develop the ability to absorb and appreciate all types of hallucinogenic stimuli.* Once you develop the ability to apply beneficial frames to your perceptions, you can alter your internal state to best fit each situation.

• • •

Don't fight negative emotions; allow yourself to experience them. Taking a small taste of the negative

---

[12] This healthy frame will greatly improve your character's Emotional Recovery, which determines how quickly your character regains composure after losing emotional control.

emotion makes you aware of what you're feeling. *Defining your feelings is the first step towards transforming them.*

RELIGIOUS HALLUCINATIONS

Many religious experiences can be derived from our ancestor's explorations into altered states of consciousness. Being able to access specific states of consciousness at will is nearly impossible[13], so rituals were developed as a tool to induce such states.

These rituals succeeded in altering our ancestor's states of consciousness because as animals[14] we have been programmed to have an external locus of control: to react to our external environment. *Traditions and rituals[15] serve as a way to create the unbounded conviction required to bestow humans with*

---

[13] The only way to induce internal states at will is by utilizing hallucinogenic ideas.

[14] Unlike any other animal, humans are gifted with the power of self-deception, which we use to convince ourselves into believing that we are humans (not animals). Perhaps our ability to be empowered by good hallucinations is what separates us from animals and makes us human after all.

[15] Rituals can also function as reminders to be mindful of the Hallucinogenic Reality.

irrational powers. The idea of God, the epitome of power, allows humans to better rule over themselves by creating an all-powerful, benevolent figure with an external locus of control. With God by their side, no other form of external control has an impact, because "the most powerful" form of external control is protecting them.

Upon closer inspection, irrational powers are not irrational. Religion is the summation of the hallucinogenic thoughts and deeply held beliefs that allow a character to better interact with themselves and the physical world.

• • •

Incarnation is the embodiment of abstract concepts. Jesus Christ, who was literally attached to a symbol of an abstract concept, was only able to withstand being nailed to the cross because he was in an altered state of consciousness that released him from the external world. The story of Christ epitomizes the power of hallucinogenic ideas — he was self-possessed by a hallucination that empowered him with the strength to endure intolerable pain. The greatest stories create a "secondary world that your mind can enter and believe is real while you are inside of it."[16] Great stories are so immersive because they often reveal hidden truths about our character's own story, causing us to identify with and project ourselves into the characters in the story. The more hallucinogenic a story is, the more others will believe it. The more characters believe in a story the more they will be influenced by it.

• • •

We can either submit to, wrestle with, or embrace the Hallucinogenic Reality. The three Abrahamic religions tell the same story from three different perspectives — they each tell the story of how humans can have a relationship with the Hallucinogenic Reality.

Islam
Submitting to the Hallucinogenic Reality.
ISLAM MOTTO: "Lose yourself in the moment!"

---

[16] Clute, John & John Grant, eds., *The Encyclopedia of Fantasy*, St Martin's, New York, 1997, article on J.R.R. Tolkien. Page 132.

Judaism

Debating whether to be a spectator of or a participant in the Hallucinogenic Reality.

JEWISH MOTTO: "To observe the moment or to live in the moment?"

Christianity

Always being aware of the Hallucinogenic Reality.

CHRISTIAN MOTTO: "Be aware of the moment."

Islamists *submit to and flow* with the Hallucinogenic Reality. Characters that are consistently attached to the Hallucinogenic Reality are unknowingly practicing the central tenet of Islam.

Jews *wrestle with and question* the Hallucinogenic Reality. Characters that fluctuate between being attached to the Hallucinogenic Reality and being non-reactive to the Hallucinogenic Reality are unknowingly practicing the central tenet of Judaism.

Christians *embrace and appreciate* the Hallucinogenic Reality. Characters that are consistently non-reactive to the Hallucinogenic Reality are unknowingly practicing the central tenet of Christianity.

Even characters who don't identify as religious stand to gain by learning how people try-on and embody abstract concepts.

THE ABSTRACT WARDROBE

The abstract qualities, thoughts, beliefs, and persona that a character presents to others.

Your first impression of a stranger introduces you to their Abstract Wardrobe. A character with a bland Abstract Wardrobe is the type of character to unquestionably abide and comply with unnecessary, outdated social contracts.[17] A character with a colorful Abstract Wardrobe is the type of character that is free enough to make fun of the pleasantry dance that most characters force themselves into complying with.[18]

---

[17] In a culture composed of characters with bland Abstract Wardrobes, social contracts are constructed to cause characters to posture as perfect versions of themselves. Those that aspire to be perfect bind themselves in an inescapable dilemma. If they succeed, everyone dislikes them for being perfect; if they fail, everyone dislikes them for not being who they said they were.

[18] In a culture composed of characters with colorful Abstract Wardrobes, unwritten rules dictate that everyone is given the freedom to be human — empowering characters with the freedom to express themselves without holding them to some arbitrary standard.

Acting in accordance with antiquated social contracts diminishes our brain's processing power and critical thinking skills. Each antiquated social contract you comply with reinforces a conditioned behavior and limits your choices. Social contracts are a form of mass hallucination that force people to self-police, causing robotized human behavior to become more prevalent than ever.[19]

If a society forces its populace to self-police, they will resent themselves and those around them.

A society that excessively polices the citizenry is a society that is disdained by the citizenry.

Force is an unnecessary, barbaric, and counterproductive tool. A more effective way to actualize a society's potential is to incentivize the populace to do what is beneficial for society. Just as each society wishes for its populace to desire the best for society, each populace clamors for a society that makes it plausible for each individual to actualize their own potential. *Actualizing your character's potential changes the world for the better by creating a rippling*

---

[19] Of course some social contracts can be beneficial. If it saves time, stops inauthenticity, and fosters collaboration the social contract may be worth keeping.

effect — having a positive affect on others contributes to the creation of a pleasant environment.[20]

Before a character can actualize their potential, they must understand who they are underneath the obfuscating layers of their Abstract Wardrobe.

---

[20] The more pleasant the environment, the more productive those inhabiting it will be. We are all responsible for our contributions to the environment.

THE ABSTRACT BODY

We are each a totally unique synthesis of abstract concepts[21] fused together to operate a biological body in the most effective way we can imagine.

Sometimes the Abstract Body is held even more privately than the physical body. Many characters wouldn't feel comfortable telling a random stranger their deepest desires and dreams, but would be comfortable sharing the most intimate parts of their body. Just like revealing your naked body, revealing your Abstract Body has the potential to make you feel vulnerable. Allowing yourself to be vulnerable allows you to enjoy freedom.

If I got a glimpse inside at who you really are, would I see a raging fire or a dwindling candle?

---

[21] Abstract concepts are the hallucinogenic stories, theories, beliefs, ideals, inspirations, motives, incentives, dreams, desires, values, principles, morals, and attitudes that a character embodies.

35

Your Abstract Body determines the power of the fire that you forge with. The Abstract Body animates the physical body: we each incarnate an abstract set of ideas and ideals that propel us through life.

The core values that construct your Abstract Body function like the systems of your physical body.

CONSCIOUSNESS & REFLECTIVENESS

Self-consciousness — the experience of being totally immersed in negative thoughts about yourself — inhibits characters from immersing themselves in an experience. Most self-conscious feelings, like pride, guilt, shame, envy, and embarrassment are bad hallucinations. The side effects of self-consciousness include anxiety, insecurity, and a general sense of discomfort.

A character that becomes self-conscious stops performing on the world stage and becomes aware of the performance. Then they act as an audience member, watching and critiquing their own performance.

In order to transform self-consciousness from a weakness into a strength, allow yourself to become a character that's aware of the Hallucinogenic Reality. Self-consciousness occurs when we are unaware that we are focusing our attention inwards. Completely immerse yourself in becoming self-reflective about being self-conscious.

Self-consciousness is like shining a light inside your imagination and being blinded by the light.

Self-reflectiveness is like shining a light on your inner mirror and reflecting that light onto the outer world so you can see the truth.

The ability to be aware that you are focusing your attention inwards allows you to readjust and focus your attention outwards.

Self-consciousness is being unaware that you are hyper-focusing on yourself. Self-consciousness breeds self-obsession. Self-obsession causes inhibited behavior.

Self-reflectiveness is being aware of the causes behind your character's thoughts, emotions, and actions. Self-reflectiveness creates self-awareness. Self-awareness enables uninhibited behavior.

Self-consciousness is like being caught in a thunderstorm of your own creation. Appreciating your experiences will transform terrifying mental storms into heavenly light shows.

IMMERSION & DETACHMENT

Attention is the foundation of all other senses. Improving our interactions with the Hallucinogenic Reality requires becoming aware of how we are focusing our attention.

TOTAL IMMERSION:

Boiling point - <u>what a character can't help but focus on.</u>

When a character is boiling, odds are they are being emotionally puppeteered by another character. Characters with low boiling points can't help but become transfixed by a situation or hallucinogenic stimuli. Those with low boiling points are susceptible to being angered and emotionally puppeteered by others. When someone's attention is completely absorbed, they are more likely to behave unconsciously, become reactive, and behave in an automated fashion. If your attention is completely immersed, your responses to the Hallucinogenic Reality will become substantially amplified.

Characters with high boiling points are able to remain unfazed when other characters are attempting to provoke them. The best leaders, performers, and athletes don't boil over, they control their boiling and use it to their advantage. In this controlled-yet-altered state, characters with high boiling points are able to perform at levels far beyond what they thought they were capable of. The next time you sense that you are about to boil over, you will instantly become aware of the moment and simmer down.

TOTAL DETACHMENT:

Freezing point - what a character cannot focus on.

High freezing points lead to shortened attention spans and prevent characters from exploring concepts they aren't familiar with. The higher your freezing point, the less of a desire you have to encounter new perspectives.

The lower your freezing point is, the more able you are to focus on things deep beneath the surface level. Those with low freezing points are able to focus on a vast array of topics and be fully engaged in what they are doing. Developing the ability to focus on self-reflection will lower your freezing point. The next time you sense that you are about to freeze over, you will notice the chill and warm yourself back up.

• • •

The higher your boiling point is and the lower your freezing point is, the more emotional control[22] you have.

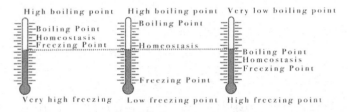

The more emotional control you have, the more proficient your coping skills are.

In the illustration above, Character 2 is the only character out of the three that has the effective coping skills to deal with this specific temperature of attention. Character 1's freezing point is so high, they freeze when experiencing this temperature of attention, and Character 3's boiling point is so low, they boil over.

---

[22] Emotional Control = your character's ability to stay composed and nonreactive when confronted with hallucinogenic stimuli.

Everyone is like a faucet. We each have different temperature extremes. Some faucets are ornate and beautiful, but get hot too fast and are never warm; some are simple but always deliver the perfect temperature.

Who you are with determines what your environment is like and what your environment is like determines what you are like — unless you are aware that everyone is like a faucet.

SPENCER GOLD

<u>Part 2:</u>
IMPLEMENTATION

GOVERNING IMAGINATIONS

A Hallucination represents your character's mental government, which structures and directs your character's Imagination.

E ach character's Imagination shines a light on their Hallucination. The puppeteered letters that compose each Hallucination cast shadows that unite

and form a new entity. This amalgamated shadow —
the Government — reflects the parts that compose it.

*A Nation's Government and a Character's
Hallucination share similar qualities but exist at
different scales in different dimensions.*

A Nation's Government = Shared Macrocosm

A Character's Hallucination = Personal Microcosm

Imagination	≈	Citizenry, how much energy is produced
Hallucination	≈	Government, how the energy is organized
Discrimination	≈	Border Patrol, how the energy conserves itself
Incarnation	≈	Culture, how the energy interacts with other energies

Each character has an internal election to decide which Hallucination will govern their Imagination. The mental government that a character elects is determined by their first principles, which includes their explanation for existence, conceptual model of the universe, idea of consciousness, justification for life's suffering, thought structuring process, etc.[23] *Each character's elected mental government contributes to the constitution of the Hallucinogenic Reality.*

The Mental Government you elect determines the pattern of your character's consciousness, which determines your conscience. The conscience is the appointed voice(s)[24] of authority ensconced within the mental government, bestowed with the exclusive responsibility to guide the Imagination. We can either unintentionally elect a Hallucination that serves someone besides us or we can intentionally elect a Hallucination that serves our Imagination.

The Imagination represents the citizenry and produces the energy needed to propel the body ahead. Even though the Hallucination is supposed to protect the Imagination, the Imagination must also always be able to protect itself from the Hallucination.

---

[23] See back of book to fill out your own internal election ballot.

[24] Depending on the results from your internal election ballot, your conscience may be singular/monarchical, dualistic/two-party system, pluralistic /democratic, etc.

A Hallucination of the Imagination, by the Imagination, for the Imagination.

The Imagination must also be able to protect itself from foreign Hallucinations. This is why each character has a Discrimination — a boundary with a mental border patrol — that separates your Hallucination from foreign Hallucinations. Mental border patrols prevent your character from being influenced by unhealthy frames.

If another character crosses over your border and invades your nation, how is your border patrol going to react? Do you allow the strangers from a foreign Hallucination to infiltrate your mental territory? Do you realize you are being invaded, panic, and not know what to do? Or do you nonchalantly take care of business and secure the border? The way you respond to a border dispute determines the rules of engagement now and in the future.

Enforcing one's borders is necessary: borders dictate what takes place inside a Hallucination. A character with stable borders has high morale and high confidence. A character with unstable borders has low morale and low confidence. Because they lack a discriminative faculty, characters with unstable borders also lack the evaluative skills needed to distinguish friend from foe.[25] The borders you construct around yourself determine the Abstract Wardrobe that you present to others. Just as an outfit can inflate or deflate a character's confidence, an Abstract Wardrobe can bring out the best or worst parts of a character's Abstract Body.

Every character has a mental border patrol that exists to protect their self-concept from potential threats.

When we are confronted by new information that directly contradicts previously held convictions, we experience cognitive dissonance — the unpleasant feeling that arises when our self-concept is destabilized. Cognitive dissonance signals an opportunity to experience growth.

Getting stuck between resistance and yielding leads to suffering. You can either correct the behavior, permit the behavior, or grant yourself the permission to express both the resistance and the yielding.

---

[25] The more unstable a characters borders are, the more defensive and easily triggered they will be.

Rather than looking at cognitive dissonance as a problem, choose to perceive it as a boiling down process that allows you to hone in on the source of the problem. What would change if the problem was solved? If the solution to a problem doesn't change anything, does the problem actually exist? Or is the hallucinated problem the problem itself?

• • •

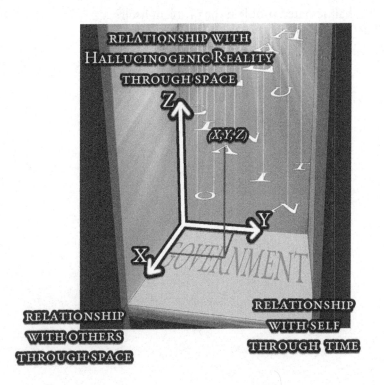

Key	Macroscopic Scale	Microscopic Scale
Light source	Citizenry's energy output	Character's Imagination
Puppeteered letter	Groups of citizens consumed in a mass hallucination	One of a character's core values
All of the puppeteered letters	Citizenry's shared Hallucination	Character's personal Hallucination
Shadow cast from individual letter	Group of citizen's shared Discrimination	Consequences resulting from having a core value
New shadow formed from composite of individual shadows	Nation's government	Character's mental government
An individual letter's frame of reference.	Group of citizen's shared culture	Culture of a character's core value
The frames of reference of all letters	Nation's shared culture	Character's Incarnation

Throughout your life, your *character's frames of reference*[26] *will change, altering the Abstract Body that you incarnate.*

Your character's frame of reference is determined by your character's *Three Relationships*:

X — Your relationship with other characters.

Y — Your relationship with your character.

Z — Your relationship with the Hallucinogenic Reality.[27]

Your *Three Relationships* determine your character's frame of reference, which determines what your character experiences and contributes.

---

[26] A reference frame or frame of reference is defined as:

1. "a set of ideas or facts that a person accepts and that influences the person's behavior, opinions, or decisions.

2. A frame of reference is also a system of lines and clocks that you can use to measure the position and motion of a set of objects and events in relation to each other."

(Cambridge Dictionary)

[27] X represents your character's harmony or pathos, Y represents your character's melody or ethos, Z represents your texture or logos.

The greater your relationship is with other characters through space, the further on the X axis your character is from the origin point, and the more *harmonious* your experiences will be. The greater your relationship is with your character through time, the further on the Y axis your character is from the origin point, and the more *meaningful* your experiences will be. The greater your relationship is with the Hallucinogenic Reality, the further on the Z axis your character is from the origin point, and the more *momentous* your experiences will be.

FRAMING REALITY

Whenever two characters both apply a competitive frame and have conflicting interpretations and judgements about a situation, there is a contest of narratives, a *Frame Clash* — an invisible border dispute between frames. The most stable frame prevails, claiming the disputed territory. When a character claims disputed territory they are subtly deciding, for all parties involved, how that interaction and all others like it will be conducted in the future.[28]

Frames compete to become the mutually accepted narrative.

The following illustration is a clip, or sequence of frames. Like frames of a filmstrip, frames of reality evolve through time. You can imagine each frame as a different response.

---

[28] These petty power games are typically unnecessary and not beneficial, but understanding their mechanics allows you to overcome them.

Frame Clash: The more stable frame absorbs the less stable frame and becomes the mutually agreed narrative.

E a c h   f r a m e   i s   a
m o m e n t ,   a c t i o n ,   o r   r e s p o n s e

F r a m e s   t r a n s i t i o n
t h r o u g h   t i m e

Frame 1 = Character 1: "I bet you a dollar you'll miss the next shot."

Frame 2 = Character 2: "Sorry, I don't take any bets under five dollars."

Frame 3 = Character 1: *laughs*

Frame 4 = Character 2: "I'll tell you what — you sink it, and I'll give you twenty."

Frame 5 = Character 1: "You're on."

Frame 6 = Character 2: "Okay, so come here and try."

Frame 7 = Character 1: *misses shot*

When a frame clash occurs, frames function like plants being bred together: the dominant frame will remain. As Gregor Mendel states in his Law of Dominance, "in a cross of parents that are pure for contrasting traits, only one form of the trait will appear in the next generation. Offspring that are hybrid for a trait will have only the dominant trait in the phenotype."

The most talented framers of reality do not engage with those that play zero-sum games.[29] The objective of framing reality is not to win the battle of perceptions by imposing your frame on others. The objective of framing reality is to transcend the battle of perceptions by applying a collaborative frame instead of a competitive frame.

All forms of communication are forms of framing.

Framing is the art of intentionally eliciting aesthetic experiences.

---

[29] Only those that are able to transcend the primitive desire to wield power over others are worthy of being bestowed with power.

*Communication is the art of eliciting responses
that you intend to elicit.*

The power of framing provides us the ability to take a peek behind the curtain and catch a glimpse into the inner workings of the Hallucinogenic Reality.

FRAMES

Frames are hallucinations that alter perceptions,
determining subjective experiences.

Perception Frames: All frames are *Perception Frames*. Perceptions function as the content, frames function as the context, and our experience functions as the subtext. Frames alter our experience of reality by contextualizing our perceptions.

The only way humans can experience reality is by applying *Perception Frames*, just like how a scuba diver, deep underwater, can only see and breathe if they're using goggles and an oxygen tank. Without *Perception Frames,* the human experience ceases to exist.

Currency Frames: Just as a nation has its own currency or as a human has its own bloodstream, an Abstract Body has its own *Currency Frame*. Characters with a strong *Currency Frame* can expect to decrease their exports of attention and to increase their imports of attention. Characters with a weak *Currency Frame* can expect to increase their exports of attention and to decrease their imports of attention.

Understand the advantages and disadvantages of strong and weak *Currency Frames* by soldering these three associations in your mind:

Nation = Character
Exports = Talking
Imports = Listening

When a nation/character is exporting/talking they are giving to take; when a nation/character is importing/listening they are taking to give. For a nation/character to present themselves to others as they wish to be perceived, they must maintain a balance of trade. A nation/character that exports/talks too much is perceived as a greedy chatterbox, dismantling other's trust in their quality of exports/words. A nation/character that imports/listens too much is perceived as a gluttonous mute; dismantling others trust in their desire to import/listen. The strongest nations/characters are capable of balancing trade. Only a character that can balance exports/talking with imports/listening has a stable *Currency Frame*.

Just as no other nation can manufacture Italian sports cars better than the Italians, no other character can offer the same exports at the same quality as your character. *A character's exports can also represent the hallucinogenic stimuli they emit, which determines the effect that character has on others. A character's imports can also represent the hallucinogenic stimuli they receive, which determines the effect others have on that character.* That is to say, the hallucinogenic stimuli your character imports affects the hallucinogenic stimuli that your character exports.

The influence you allow others to have on you determines the influence you have on others.

PREFRAMES

Preframes[30] prime others to respond to your character in a specific way. Your character's preframe largely determines the type of hallucinogenic effect that you have on others.

Preframers cause others to endow them with qualities they want to be associated with. Like any convincing illusion, Preframes manipulate perceptions.

Fabrication is a type of preframe. Erving Goffman, the prestigious sociologist who developed frame theory, wrote, "fabrication [...] is based [...] on deceit."[31] When characters alter their appearance, they are engaging in fabrication. Costuming, makeup, hairstyling, and voice alteration are all methods of fabrication. Characters use fabrication to alter their

---

[30] Preframes are stories that characters present to others that dictate how other characters react to them. Preframes are mostly nonverbal cues such as a character's posture, stature, and presence that reveal how that character will act and react, and how others will act and react to them.

[31] Goffman, E. (1974). Frame analysis: An essay on the organization of experience.

presence and construct a preframe that elicits desired responses from others.

The fashion industry appears as the leader of Fabrication, but the most elite positions of society are the ones who truly excel in the art. The judge wears a robe that primes others to treat them as an authority figure. The doctor wears a white lab coat that primes others to treat them as a credible source. Businessmen wear suits to prime others to treat them with dignity and respect. Police officers wear uniforms to prime others to treat them professionally and courteously. In a world where everyone engages in fabrication, even those that choose not to consciously take part are still fabricating — their fabrication is just minimal, planned messiness, with the intention to prime others to see them as relatable, humble, and trustworthy. Fabricators attempt to and often succeed at winning the battle of perceptions before others even have time to realize that a battle has begun. Fabricators engage in the battle of perceptions to weave their own fabric of reality — to make their frame the mutually accepted frame.

Italicization is a closeup, drawing the attention of other characters to a specific thing to convey a certain meaning. Italicization can be physical or verbal.

When physical, Italicization is a type of fabrication where one part of a character's ensemble is especially attention-grabbing. Italicization causes others to associate you with a specific aesthetic. When verbal, Italicization is used to emphasize what one character wants other characters to focus their attention on.

An example of the Italicizing preframe is a character's name: names are among the first things that you learn about a person. If a character's name doesn't preframe them in a positive light, it isn't a good name. Other examples of Italicizing preframes include job titles, online usernames, and voices.

Professions that excel in utilizing Italicization include Politicians, Hypnotists, Preachers, Lawyers, Motivational Speakers, Public Intellectuals, Broadcasters, and any other Talented Speaker that is easily able to focus an audience's attention.

Value Frames prescribe worth. Value Frames are hallucinogenic stories that — when mutually agreed upon — dictate price.

Assigning a price to a commodity, like an art piece, reveals that the most basic form of value is determined by the experience provided by that commodity's hallucinogenic stimuli.

Value Frames alter a character's experience of a hallucinogenic stimuli by priming their expectations. What we expect to happen is more likely to happen because our expectations cause us to selectively perceive what we expect. Expectancy can also amplify our responses to hallucinogenic stimuli by building anticipation.

All Value Frames are dependent on credit. The word "credit" is derived from the Latin "credere," which means "believe, trust."[32] Money lenders are only credible if the borrower believes they can trust them. If a character does not have faith in the value of another character's or institution's word, they will not trust what they have to say, let alone give them their money.

The greatest experiences are far more valuable than the greatest products. Products merely attempt to deliver experiences. Products have a price; experiences are priceless. Professions that excel in utilizing Value Frames include: Scientists, Bankers, Economists, Advertisers, Artists, Salesmen, Journalists, and Consultants.

Scoring determines movement, attitude, and mood. A character's Score preframes how an

---

[32] Oxford University Press, *Lexico Dictionaries,* 2019

interaction will be conducted, just as background music informs the audience what to feel about a scene in a film. If you can imagine changing the musical Score to your character's life, you can change your character's emotions, thoughts, and actions. Professions that excel in utilizing Scoring include: Negotiators, Athletes, Comedians, Actors, Musicians, and all sorts of Opinion Leaders.

Hierarchization assigns each character to a role in an ordered position. Hierarchization determines the role that you occupy, and the role that you occupy determines what other characters expect of you. Hierarchies exist because they prevent unnecessary power struggles by preemptively deciding who bears each responsibility.

Hierarchization causes most characters to become fully immersed in their assigned roles. Characters that are totally immersed in an experience forget that they are experiencing something, forget who they are, and lose themselves in the role that they are playing. Professions that excel in utilizing Hierarchization include: Doctors, World Leaders, C-Suite Executives, Military Generals, and all sorts of Professional

Organizations that are ordered and organized based on rank.

DEFRAMES

Deframes deconstruct frames and preframes so that they can be reconstructed into more beneficial frames.

Deframes utilize the hallucinogens "shock, surprise, confusion, doubt, dissociation, disequilibrium [because they] are all means of depotentiating patients' learned limitations so that they become open and available for new means of experiencing and learning..."[33] Deframes deconstruct frames and reconstruct them. *Taking something apart and not replacing it with a more effective version defeats the purpose of taking it apart.*

When a character tries to frame an event by communicating, "what you're saying is so *this*," you can deframe their frame by saying, "not quite, what I'm saying is, in fact, *that*, and we both know you love *that*." Deframes make *this* about *that*.

---

[33] Erickson and Rossi, Hypnotic Realities, pg 205

Denying: "No you're wrong." Denying someone is a simple way to communicate that the current frame doesn't exist. The phrases "no," "incorrect," "not true," "wrong," and "fake," are all forms of Denying deframes. However, Denial is probably the most ineffective form of deframing because it directly responds to the opposing frame.

Why would you respond directly to an opposing frame? Doing so limits your options and destabilizes your frame while stabilizing the opposing frame. If an attempted deframe stabilizes the opposing frame, it's not only an ineffective deframe, it's a self-sabotaging deframe.

Degrading: "Don't be an idiot." Degradation intends to instantly deframe. By Degrading a character, you deframe them and reframe them with a new frame of your own. Degrading others attracts those that identify as winners, but distances you from those that identify as empathetic. Be wary of overusing Degrading deframes.[34]

---

[34] Degrading deframes can be cast with a playful intention or domineering intention. Some characters may attempt to pass off their domineering intentions as playful intentions, but playful intentions and domineering intentions are clearly distinguishable.

Deconstructing: "I know what you're doing." Deconstructing deframes disassemble a proposition "typically in order to expose its hidden internal assumptions and contradictions and subvert its apparent significance or unity."[35] Deconstructing deframes don't emphatically tear down like Degrading deframes, Deconstructing deframes dissects the whole into its pieces to analyze how they function and can be reinterpreted or repurposed. Like a river gradually carving out a canyon, Deconstructing deframes persistently sculpt the substratum of subtext.

Dismissing: "That's not important." Dismissive methods intend to make the current frame frivolous. The most commonly used Dismissive deframe is simply responding in a way that doesn't acknowledge that frame. For example, Dismissing another character's Degradation communicates that the Degrading character cannot deframe your frame. Characters that attempt to provoke reactions cannot

---

[35] Oxford University Press, *Lexico Dictionaries,* 2019

affect you if you nonchalantly Dismiss their frame.[36]

Decoupling: "These two things are not connected." The intention of a Decoupling deframe is to change a character's — or your own — behavior from its usual context to improve their/your response to the content. By Decoupling content from context, a character is able to choose how to recontextualize the content and develop more beneficial behavior. If you continually behave in an unbeneficial manner when faced with a certain type of content, a Decoupling deframe will enable you to alter your automatic response to the content.

---

[36] If a character reacts to your dismissive deframe by becoming aggressive, don't dismiss their hostility and don't acknowledge their aggression; doing so will only make them more aggressive. To disarm an aggressive provocateur, communicate with analogies. Analogical communication disarms the aggressive by indirectly causing them to look inwards. By speaking about the antagonist analogically, you enable them to observe their actions and sober up from their trance-like state. Analogical communication works because it conveys meaning without being taken personally, preventing the aggressive from lashing out.

MISFRAMES

Misframes are hallucinations that are imposed by others.

Misframes are rhetorical techniques that portray characters in an inaccurate and unscrupulous way. Those that misframe others are projecting their mental image onto other characters, discounting that character's own mental image in the process.[37] Projecting your idea of others onto them should only be done thoughtfully, playfully, and ethically, because the way a character truly sees themselves has a great impact on determining who that character actually is. If a character is misframed as someone they don't

---

[37] Those that have been misframed are often compelled to misframe others. Misframes not only manipulate the perceptions of the group, misframes erode the misframed character's faith in their own perception of reality. Those that have no faith in their own perception of reality lose the ability to define their emotions because they believe that they would be too painful to feel. If a character can't define their emotions they will be unable to know themselves. If a character doesn't know who they are they will be insecure. If they are insecure they will be resentful. If they are resentful they will be cruel and misframe others. Misframers do this because they can only determine their value by comparing themselves to others, so if others are doing poorly they feel better about themselves.

believe they are, that character will feel compelled to fight the foreign frame imposed on them.

Rather than react defensively and fall into the frame of the character misframing you, choose to drop back and focus on how the misframer is trying to manipulate everyone's perceptions, including your own.

The five keys needed to reclaim your character after being misframed are neutrality, patience, pleasantness, understanding, and empathy.

Typically, if a character discovers that someone else is manipulating everyone's perceptions of the event, they become angry and lash out.[38] But by lashing out, that character loses the battle of perceptions and falls into the misframer's frame. Neutrality and patience slow your character's descent to anger, which prevents you from falling into a misframing character's inaccurate frame.

When the truth is unknown, perceptions take the place of truth. When hallucinations are unaccounted

---

[38] Those that need to have numbers on their side to win the battle of perceptions have an unstable frame. A hyena is only willing to confront a lion if they have support from other hyenas.

for, hallucinated authority becomes actual authority. For your character to win the battle of perceptions, calmly diffuse the misframer's smokescreen of lies in a pleasant but direct way. If you are understanding and empathetic, the character misframing you doesn't have the power to upset you — they only felt the need to misframe your character because their own frame is unstable.

Most characters automatically react in a defensive way and try to shut down those that misframe them. If a misframer manages to erode a character's faith in their perception of reality, that character stops defining who they are for themselves and starts defining themselves based on the other character's definitions of them. Many unnecessarily fall into this trap due to the unhealthy characters they are surrounded by.[39] A character with a stable frame is immune to gaslighting.

Misinterpretation: the most common type of misframe is a Misinterpretation. Misinterpretations can be both accidental and intentional. The vast majority of Misinterpretations are accidental.

---

[39] Gaslighters attempt to make others doubt their perception of reality, so that they can control the outcome or conclusion of the situation.

Characters that Misinterpret others usually have negative reactions. Characters that habitually behave in a particular way tend to be accused of acting that way, even if they aren't. Characters often Misinterpret others because they are making assumptions without any evidence to substantiate their claims. Characters may also Misinterpret others if they personally dislike them[40]. On the other hand, most intentional Misinterpretations are benign.

Misdirection: If a character who is guilty of something is accused of being guilty, and they accuse their accuser of committing the crime they just committed, they are using a Misdirectional misframe. When confronting a character for projecting bad hallucinations, expect to encounter Misdirection. The Misdirector will often accuse you of projecting, even though they are actually the ones projecting.

Mislabelling: "This is who you are." Mislabels are a quick and dirty way for characters to convince themselves and others that the character being labelled is not worth listening to. Mislabels project a false image

---

[40] Characters often dislike those that express a repressed part of themselves.

onto a character, altering the perceptions others have about that character. Those that fall for Mislabels are just as much of the problem as those that Mislabel others.

Misassociation: "You're like this." Misassociation is another common variation of misframe because they can be applied to both characters and ideas. Those that make Misassociations tend to make sweeping generalizations or inaccurate comparisons to persuade others of a point that is untrue.

REFRAMES

Reframes change the conduct of interactions by altering your character's perception with good hallucinations.

Unlike deframes, reframes do not change *this* into *that*; reframes change what *this* is.

Zooming: Everyone naturally focuses on the big picture before they focus on the details. Zoom in and magnify what is beneficial for you to focus on. Being aware of what you are zoomed in on allows you to refocus your attention. Zooming is the act of relating parts to the sum in order to create a more beneficial model of reality, or story of the situation.

Spaceframing: a physical Spaceframe limits a character's movement. The most obvious example of a physical Spaceframe is a prison, where the inmates are told where they are allowed to move and when. House arrest is another example of physical Spaceframing that restricts movement and access. Other types of physical Spaceframing range from national borders to waiting rooms.

While many Spaceframes are necessary, like roads, some of them, like V.I.P. sections at clubs, are frivolous and only exist to limit one group's access in order to make another group feel more important. In order to overcome Spaceframing, learn to be at peace with what you can and cannot control, and make the best of whatever situation you are placed in — while respecting the Spaceframes that are necessary, such as private property.

Spaceframes can also be mental. Characters that trap themselves in a mental Spaceframe are experiencing a bad hallucination. This tricks those characters into believing they're kind, when in actuality they're just smarmy. Many of the characters that are confined in mental Spaceframes have experienced an event in their life that caused them to filter their actions, thoughts, and feelings. By filtering themselves, these unfortunate characters have lost their ability to leverage their instincts.

Spaceframes can also combine the physical and the mental; the epitome of which is money. Money determines a character's ability to travel where they please and determines their access to the resources they need — let alone desire. Money dictates each character's environment, lifestyle, and possessions, which have a cascading effect on thoughts, emotions, and states of consciousness.

Timeframing: If a character demands that something be done at a certain time, they are controlling the Timeframe of the event. Institutions are dependent on Timeframing; without them, everyone's schedules could not be synchronized.

Timeframing is a subtle display of power that can control an entire interaction. To prevent your character from being Timeframed, use a Dismissing deframe by responding without acknowledging the Timeframe. By embracing this choice, your character becomes immersed in a good hallucination and is empowered.

Money is also often dependent on Timeframing. By quantifying a character's time into a fixed hourly rate, money becomes the physical manifestation of a Timeframe.

Keying: "Keying is a more creative process where [frame] transformation can take place through make believe, sport, games, ritual, experimentation, practice.[41] Keying is also a video editing tool that

---

[41] Goffman, E. (1974). Frame analysis: An essay on the organization of experience.

removes and substitutes the background with a new one so the character in the foreground can be placed in a more desirable scene. For example, if your character is stuck in a chair having a tooth drilled at the dentist, you can use a keying frame to diminish the pain. Imagine that you are no longer at the dentist, imagine that you have been teleported to the beach on a beautiful summer day. Those that are able to truly believe that they are at the beach — those that are able to convince themselves into feeling the sun shine on their hair, the sand in-between their toes — are able to be at peace even when the dentist is drilling.

Keying changes the scene your character is in, which alters how your character feels, thinks, and acts. Those that are able to key in real time are masters at utilizing good hallucinations to their advantage. Keying is like teleporting your character into a parallel universe, untethering from one context and attaching to another.

This type of reframe is most easily used by those that wish to avoid immersion in the situations they experience.

Those that are routinely put in scenes that they would like to escape from naturally develop the ability to use keying reframes. For this reason, anxious characters may actually have an easier time keying a situation than a character that isn't anxious, because anxious characters have more experience untethering themselves from situations. To key in real life, characters can use narration or visualization: describing and experiencing what is happening in a scene. Keying is one of the most powerful types of reframes because it bestows a character with the power to reframe their experiences in the most beneficial way imaginable.

Keyframing is a method to arrive at the future by predicting which actions will result in which outcomes. Keyframing is another video editing tool that allows your character to cue up responses and create smooth transitions from frame to frame. Master Keyframers are able to know other characters intimately from just a first impression. Some are even able to see the entirety of a character's arc just by meeting them in person.

A Keyframer's greatest strength is their ability to subtly lead interactions by seamlessly transitioning between experiences. Doing so allows the Keyframer to create a sequence of actions with a specific outcome — simply by making one action in advance.

MAKE YOUR TABLE

Frames are constructed like tables. If your table is missing a leg, it won't be stable. Each conscious belief functions as a tabletop, and *each of your subconscious beliefs function as a leg that supports that tabletop.* The more congruent your character's subconscious belief is with your conscious belief, the more stable your frame.

Believing only one frame should survive is like standing atop your table, looking down, and boasting about how supreme you are. When everyone is yelling from atop their tables, take a seat and calmly remind them that tables serve a better purpose than as a soapbox.

Instead of standing atop your table, why not sit down, make your table, and enjoy eating in peace?

Each time they try to dismiss you and continue posturing, you will even further enjoy the comfort of sitting down. Those who are able to sit down and eat in peace in the presence of a character who is ranting and raving atop their table are developing the skills they need to be great leaders.

Paradoxically, the one frame that dominates all other frames is the frame that allows other frames to exist.[42] Tyrants attempt to squish every other frame that isn't working under their control, and cannot afford to be generous. Great leaders are generous, unthreatened by other frames, and encourage others to reinforce what works for them.

Each character's frame is designed to justify their choices. Each choice stabilizes or destabilizes their self-concept. Each character frames reality in whichever way makes them feel most satisfied for doing what they want to do — we frame our reality to correspond with what's in the best interest of our self-concept. Reinforcing one's self-concept without ever questioning the nature of it is not beneficial. Doubt is a key ingredient to awaken a character from the ever-persistent hallucination that is their self-concept. Once a character stops casting the spell of their self-concept on themselves, their hallucinogenic thoughts will no longer torment them. Hallucinogenic thoughts only

---

[42] The one exception to the rule, is that it is necessary to be intolerant of those that do not tolerate the existence of other frames.

torment those that have forgotten who they are and what their purpose is.[43]

---

[43] Believing that your character has no purpose is a bad hallucination that prevents you from discovering and actualizing your purpose.

TYPES OF HALLUCINOGENIC STIMULI

All types of hallucinogenic stimuli are miracles that we take for granted.

Even the most unpleasant types of hallucinogenic stimuli exist for a purpose. Without dissonance, the greatest music ceases to exist. Unpleasantness is a necessary part of experiencing a finite existence. We exist in the Hallucinogenic Reality to experience finality for the first time[44]. Finality entails temporality which makes the experience of an emotional life possible.

---

[44] The Hallucinogenic Reality is an infinite, immortal, all-powerful entity that was barred from only one thing, the experience of finality, so it created us. The Hallucinogenic Reality created us as autonomous entities with a finite existence so that we both can experience life in all of its fullness for the first time. The Hallucinogenic Reality vicariously lives through us to enjoy our unique experience of itself.

The type of hallucinogenic stimuli that you routinely experience determines the type of hallucinogenic stimuli your character emits. We become what consumes us, unless we choose otherwise.

Desaturators

➤ Hallucinogenic stimuli that diminish a character's current emotions, thoughts, and consciousness, downplaying experiences.

  ✓ An example of a *Desaturator* is the thought "I don't care about this."

Saturators

➤ Hallucinogenic stimuli that cause a character's current emotions, thoughts, and consciousness to be exaggerated so that their experiences become more amplified. The opposite of a *Desaturator*.

  ✓ An example[45] of a *Saturator* is a crowd of people.

---

[45] Juxtaposing two disparate objects amplifies the qualities of both objects, creating a *Saturator*.

_____

Shifters[46]

➤ Hallucinogenic stimuli that completely alters a character's current emotions, thoughts, and consciousness, transforming their experience.

    ✓ An example of a *Shifter* is the sun reemerging from behind a cloud.

Types of Shifters:

Clarifiers

✳ A type of *Shifter* that attempts to cause your character to feel balanced, coherent, clear-minded, or grounded.

    ✓ An example of a *Clarifier* is a speech from a brilliant orator.

Soothers

✳ A type of *Shifter* that attempts to cause your character to become tranquil, comfortable, relaxed, trusting, recharged, and relieved of any anxiety.

_____

[46] Any *Shifter* when experienced in excess becomes a *Desaturator*.

✓ An example of a *Soother* is mellow music.

Confusers

✴ A type of *Shifter* that attempts to cause your character to feel confused, doubtful, indrawn, or disrupted.

> ✓ An example of a *Confuser* is a question that is so off-topic it distracts your character's attention and makes you forget what you were talking about.

Aggravators

✴ A type of *Shifter* that attempts to cause your character to become aggravated; annoyed, outraged, or frustrated.

> ✓ An example of an *Aggravator* is someone aggressively commanding you to "calm down," when you're already calm, just so they can help calm themselves down.
>
> ✓ The more clarified your perception of reality becomes, the less impact *Aggravators* will have.

Debasers

＊ A type of *Shifter* that attempts to cause your character to feel down, disparaged, insecure, inferior, anxious, or depressed.

✓ An example of a *Debaser* is a character that pretends to motivate others and give business advice, but is actually only giving that advice in order to present themselves as the image of the quintessential guru to their fans. *Debasers* can't let anyone else shine besides them.

Exciters

＊ A type of *Shifter* that attempts to cause your character to feel up, invigorated, energized, or socially confident.

✓ An example of an *Exciter* is a motivational speaker pumping up an entire crowd with confidence.

Amusers

✳ A type of *Shifter* that attempts to cause your character to be playful, happy, funny, creative, or intrigued.

> ✓ An example of an *Amuser* is a comedian telling a hilarious joke.

Terrifiers

✳ A type of *Shifter* that attempts to cause your character to panic or feel paranoid.

> ✓ An example of a *Terrifier* is a news headline warning people that they are in danger.

> ✓ If the source of a character's fear is not addressed, they will continue to be fearful. If the source of fear persists, an *Amuser* will chase it away.

Unsettler

✳ A type of Shifter that attempts to cause your character to become stressed, anxious, jittery, overwhelmed, neurotic, high-strung, and uneasy.

    ✓ An example of an *Unsettler* is the thought that you have to pay off a debt.

    ✓ Anxiety relieving activities are not as effecting at assuaging anxiety as joy generating activities.

———————

Reversals

➤ Hallucinogenic stimuli that reverses a character's current emotions, thoughts, and consciousness, resulting in an experience that's the exact opposite of the previous experience.

    ✓ An example of a *Reversal* is a joke that cuts the tension in the room.

———————

Continuators

➤ Hallucinogenic stimuli that causes a character's current emotions, thoughts, and consciousness to remain the same for an extended period of time.

  ✓ An example of a *Continuator* is the book *Hallucination Theory*.

HALLUCINATION THEORY

THE INTERNAL BALLOT

INSTRUCTIONS FOR TAKING THE INTERNAL BALLOT

Visit http://www.Hallucination.us to fill out your internal ballot online.

Or, fill out your own internal ballot on the following page.

Instructions on how to tally your results can be found online at http://www.Hallucination.us/Continuator

HALLUCINATION THEORY

Which Hallucinations govern your Imagination?

INTENTION

only select one

Purposeful			Random
The universe was or is being intelligently designed.	☐	☐	*The universe was spontaneously formed.*
Caused			**Uncaused**
With beginning. The universe was created in a singular moment.	☐	☐	*Without beginning. The universe has always existed.*
If caused, clear (provable) cause?			**If caused,** unclear (unprovable) cause?
It's possible to prove the initial cause of the universe.	☐	☐	*It's impossible to prove the original cause of the universe.*
Infinite			**Finite**
The universe will always exist.	☐	☐	*The universe will, someday, cease to exist.*

EXISTENCE

only select one

Dynamic			Static
The universe is changing.	☐	☐	*The universe does not change, and perpetually remains the same size.*
If changing, evolving & growing?			**If changing,** only evolving?
The universe is expanding, and changing as it grows.	☐	☐	*The universe is changing, but not expanding.*
Indestructible universe			**Destructible universe**
The universe cannot be destroyed.	☐	☐	*The universe can be destroyed.*
If destroyed, irreparably?			**If destroyed,** cyclically recreated?
Once the universe is destroyed, it cannot be recreated.	☐	☐	*The universe is cyclically created and destroyed and created again, etc.*
Sentient universe			**Inanimate universe**
The universe is a living organism, more than the sum of its parts.	☐	☐	*The universe is an ecosystem, the sum of its parts.*

CONSCIOUSNESS		
only select one		

Immortal	☐	☐	**Mortal**
Consciousness is eternal. Death is impermanent.			*Consciousness ceases to exists after life on earth. Death is permanent.*

If immortal, reincarnation?	☐	☐	**If immortal**, afterlife?
After life on earth, your consciousness inhabits a different entity to experience life anew.			*After life on earth, your consciousness reaches its final destination.*

Personal consciousness	☐	☐	**Shared consciousness**
Upwards causation. We are all unique individuals, each of us with with our own differentiated consciousness.			*Downwards causation. Individuality is an illusion. The whole controls the parts. We are all one undifferentiated consciousness.*

Experience is perception of reality	☐	☐	**Experience is reality itself**
My perception of reality is subjective.			*My perception of reality is objective.*

Conception of god	☐	☐	**No conception of God**
God(s) exist(s).			*God(s) do(es) not exist.*

If conception of god, monotheism?	☐	☐	**If conception of god**, polytheism?
Only one god exists. Denying or tolerating the existence of other deities.			*Many gods or deities exist. Intolerance is blasphemous.*

If polytheistic, holacratic polytheism?	☐	☐	**If polytheistic**, henotheism?
All deities are equal but different, no chief deity exists.			*There are many deities, with one chief deity.*

Life's suffering is justified	☐	☐	**Life's suffering has no justification**
There is a justification to explain the suffering life entails.			*There is no necessary justification to explain the suffering that life entails. Suffering is just an intrinsic part of life, and an epiphenomenon of evolution.*

If justified, moral?	☐	☐	**If justified**, aesthetic?
We are here to learn a lesson, life is like a school, we are here to evolve.			*We are here to appreciate and co-create our aesthetic experience.*

Fate	☐	☐	**Free will**
The universe predetermines our destiny.			*We choose our actions and create our own destiny.*

Historical consciousness	☐	☐	**Ahistorical consciousness**
Nature and genetics are our primary influences.			*Nurture and mental constructs are our primary influences.*

Made in the USA
Las Vegas, NV
15 June 2021